Contents

RIGBY

Halley Court, Jordan Hill, Oxford, OX2 8EJ
a division of Harcourt Education Ltd

www.myprimary.co.uk

Help and support for teachers, plus the widest range of education solutions

Rigby is a registered trademark of Harcourt Education Ltd

All Alone first published 2004

Series editor: Shirley Bickler

08 07
10 9 8 7 6 5

All Alone
ISBN 978 0433 03537 4

Group reading pack with teaching notes
ISBN 0433 035692 / 978 0433 035695

Illustrated by David Smith, Abigail Conway and David Roberts

Cover illustration © David Lupton

Designed by StoreyBooks

Repro by Digital Imaging, Glasgow

Printed and bound in China by CTPS

The Diamond Cave

scenes from RM Ballantyne's
Coral Island

adapted by William Bedford

illustrated by David Smith

Ralph, Peter and Jack had been washed ashore on Coral Island after their sailing ship, The Arrow, *smashed against a coral reef in a great storm.* The Arrow *had sunk without trace and the three friends were the only survivors. Several months later, they were still stranded on the island.*

Jack and I were searching for shellfish in the rock pools, and Peter was sunning himself on the rocks. Since being attacked by sharks, Peter was terrified of water. He kept out of the sea as much as he could and refused to dive.

Suddenly, we heard him shout, "A sail!" He was pointing excitedly.

At first, we thought he was playing one of his games. But this morning he was not joking.

"Come on, Ralph!" Jack cried, and the two of us raced up the rocks to get a better view. On the horizon, a dark smudge was moving rapidly towards us.

"Is it a sail or a cloud?" Jack wondered. We had often seen storms blow up suddenly from distant clouds.

"It *is* a sail!" I exclaimed, and we danced together on the rocks, soon joined by the excited Peter.

I'm sure the thought of home filled all our minds as we watched the vessel sail towards us.

"Wave so they see us!" cried Jack, and we waved and shouted, sure of our rescue at last.

To our delight, we saw the crew beginning to lower a rowing boat as if they meant to land. Then a little cloud of white smoke rose from the ship's side.

Before we could begin to guess the meaning of this smoke, a cannon-shot came crashing through the bushes, carrying away several trees.

It was then that we spotted the flag on the ship's main mast. With feelings of terror, we saw that it was black, with a Death's-head and cross bones upon it: the skull and cross bones.

"Pirates!" we gasped together.

"Come on," Jack said urgently. "We must hide. If they capture us, we'll be forced to walk the plank."

Jack was our leader, and we followed him without argument. Behind us, the rowing boat had reached the shore. The crew leapt overboard and rushed across the white sands in pursuit.

There were five of them, and they fired shots after us, their bullets thudding into the tall coconut trees.

We clawed our way up the cliffs overlooking the shore, and fell to the ground when we reached the top, gasping for breath. We could see the deserted beach and the rowing boat bobbing in the surf. The pirates were nowhere in sight.

When he had caught his breath, Jack gasped, "We have to escape."

"How can we?" Peter cried. "We have no way of reaching another island."

He was right. We had no boat, and it would have been impossible to swim that far.

But Jack was not listening. "Let's get away from here!" he said, and he made for the undergrowth.

We had to fight our way through the dense jungle along the edge of the cliffs. Stinging insects buzzed in the air. There was little sound apart from our heavy breathing and the high screech of parrots.

At last, we emerged from the undergrowth.

There were rocks all around us, as if left after a rockfall or earthquake. The sea thundered down below.

"I stumbled upon this place a few weeks ago," Jack said.

He led us through a maze of sandy passages between the rocks. Suddenly, we turned a corner and found ourselves standing on a narrow ledge. A sheer drop lay before us, and a deep pool that was hidden among the rocks.

I leant forward and stared down into the water.

Jack pointed. "Down there," he said quietly, "is a cave."

I looked again, surprised by his words. The water was very clear. White sand shone at the bottom of the pool. But I could see no cave.

"You see that light," Jack said. I did. There was a strange green light in the water. It shone out from the side of the rocks, about ten feet below the surface.

"That light is shining from a cave," Jack said. "I found it when I was looking for shellfish. We can dive down into the pool and swim through the entrance. Inside the cave, there is dry rock and room to hide. I've been hiding supplies there for weeks."

Peter stiffened. "I can't dive," he insisted.

Before he could say more, we heard a branch breaking, and a man's cough. "They're close," Jack whispered. "You must decide, Peter. We either dive, or stand and fight."

Peter let out a frightened laugh. The colour drained from his thin face. "I'd rather die than dive down there!" he said firmly. He began to back away. "I won't do it."

"Listen, Peter ... " I tried to say, but he glared at me in his terror.

"I told you, I can't do it!" he said desperately.

Jack looked determined. "Then we must fight," he said. "We will never leave you."

"There are five of them, Jack," I pointed out. "We haven't got a chance."

"Then we will die."

There was a brief silence. Peter took a deep breath. He was struggling to control his fear. I felt certain he would lose the struggle.

"Come on then!" he cried suddenly, the words bursting out of him.

And before we could move to stop him, he had walked to the edge of the rocks, closed his eyes, and plunged forward into the silent waters.

Jack dived in after him in less than a second, and I followed. Even as I dived, I heard the pirates crashing through the undergrowth. Another second, and they would have seen us. Then I was under water.

I swam down, following Jack. Peter was floundering in the depths. He was clearly panicking. I saw Jack seize one of Peter's arms, and I quickly seized the other.

We drew close to him on either side and kicked our legs, swimming straight for the green shimmering light.

My heart was racing. I tried to keep my eyes open, but I too was starting to panic. My lungs were bursting. Water was going up my nose, and bubbles surged around my head. I wanted to shout for help, but knew that if I opened my mouth I would drown.

Then suddenly we were in a narrow tunnel. My lungs were filling with water now, and I felt a sharp pain as my arm hit the rocks. A blinding light dazzled my eyes.

Even as I opened my mouth and felt the water rushing in, our heads were out of water. We had made it! Glorious air filled my lungs. In a few seconds, we were clambering onto a ledge of dry rock.

"Thank heavens," I heard Jack gasp.

Peter drew a long, deep breath, and slumped down onto the rocks. His face was white, his teeth chattering, his whole body shaking.

While Peter and I rested, Jack searched for the torch and tinder he had left behind on one of his earlier trips. He lit the torch, and Peter gasped at the brilliant stones in the roof of the cave.

"Are they diamonds?" he asked.

"Stones of some kind," Jack said, "but I don't know whether they're diamonds."

"I'll imagine they're diamonds," said Peter. "That makes a better story."

The torch burnt brightly, and there was food and water for several days.

We heard shouts from the pirates, and another shot from a pistol. It was probably a signal to the pirate ship. Then silence descended, and all we could hear was the distant rumble of the sea, and the cries of seabirds.

In the long stillness of night, Jack and I broke open fresh coconuts, and drank a toast of coconut milk to Peter, the bravest of all of us.

Then we put out our light, and settled down to sleep, wondering what the morning would bring us. In our pleasure at escaping, we believed the pirates had gone.

We were to find out our mistake, but that's another story ...

The Pit and the Pendulum

written by Edgar Allan Poe
adapted by Simon Cheshire

illustrated by Abigail Conway

This story is set in Spain around the year 1500. The narrator has been put in prison by the Spanish Inquisition – an organisation which tortured and killed people because of their religious beliefs.

I felt ill. Very ill. I had been put on trial. I had been sentenced to death. That was all I could remember.

The fog in my mind slowly cleared. Where was I now? Where had I been taken? For a moment, I dared not open my eyes. When I did, I could see nothing. Nothing at all.

I stretched out my hands in the darkness. Beneath me was a cold, stone floor. My clothes had been replaced with rags. The air was thick and stale.

I'd heard horrible stories about what happened to victims of the Spanish Inquisition. Had they placed me in a tomb? Sealed me up to die slowly?

Terrified, I rose and moved forward. Carefully, shuffling. At last my fingers touched the walls.

The stone was damp and slimy. This place was too big to be a tomb. A dungeon perhaps? My terror overcame me, and I collapsed.

When I awoke, I found that a loaf of bread and a jug of water had been placed beside me. I ate and drank quickly, desperate with hunger and thirst.

I finally felt more sure of myself. I decided to discover all I could about the dungeon. To begin with, I decided to walk across it, to get an idea of its size.

I stood with my back to the wall, then walked forward. In the total darkness, I had nothing to guide me but the feel of the stone floor underfoot. I'd gone no more than a few paces when the rags I was wearing caught around my ankles. I fell onto my face. And then I froze in horror. My chin had struck the hard floor, but my nose ... my nose met nothing but vile, stinking air.

The floor ended under my face! Ahead of me was a large, circular hole. I picked a broken scrap of stone from the floor and dropped it. The stone bounced off the sides of the pit. After many seconds of falling, I heard it plop into water, far below. The pit was terrifyingly deep.

I gasped in fright. My captors had clearly meant for me to fall into the pit – fall to my death!

No sooner had I escaped this awful fate, there was a sudden noise far above me. For a moment, there was a glimpse of light. Then there was a clanking sound, and the light vanished. Something had happened up there. I had no idea what it could be.

I crawled back to the dungeon walls and kept as far away from the pit as I could. What would be in store for me now? Once more, I thought about the terrible tales I'd heard about the Inquisition and its prisoners. Eventually, I slept. I don't know how long I was asleep. But when I woke up, bread and water were beside me again. I devoured them in an instant. However, I quickly regretted my haste. The water must have been drugged, for I felt myself sinking into numbness.

It is impossible to say how much time passed. When I awoke, I found myself on my back, unable to move.

And ... I could see! Dim light shone in the dungeon. So dim that I could only just make out my surroundings.

I was tied to a wooden frame. A thick leather strap was tied round me, holding me still.

My prison was large and square. Bolted to the walls were huge metal plates. On each plate were pictures: of monsters and demons and every foul thing you can imagine.

To one side of me was a dish of meat. It was just within my reach. I was about to take some when I noticed the rats.

There were dozens of them – dark and fat. They scurried out of the pit, their tails wriggling, attracted by the smell of the meat. Already they were scuttling closer.

I tried to scare them off as best I could. But then I noticed the ceiling of the dungeon, several metres above me. And it made me forget all about the rats.

On the ceiling was a picture of Old Father Time. A pendulum hung from his outstretched hand. At the bottom of it was a wide, crescent-shaped metal blade. The whole pendulum appeared to be moving.

I blinked my eyes and shook my head. I stared up at it again. There was no mistake. The pendulum was swinging. Back and forth, back and forth, in a long, slow arc. Its curved blade hissed as it cut through the stifling atmosphere of the dungeon.

So this was what the Inquisition had in store for me! Slowly, slowly, slowly, swung the pendulum. Back and forth, lower and lower, down and down towards me. For hours I watched it. Hour after

hour it swung, dropping the tiniest bit lower with each swing.

It drove me near to madness. The waiting; the watching; the terrible swinging of the blade. At last, it was only centimetres above me. The strap which held me had been carefully tied. It wound around every part of me except my chest. It was my chest that the blade would slice into.

By now, the rats had taken all but a small piece of the meat. Some of them were even biting at my fingers. It seemed they would gnaw at anything that might be food.

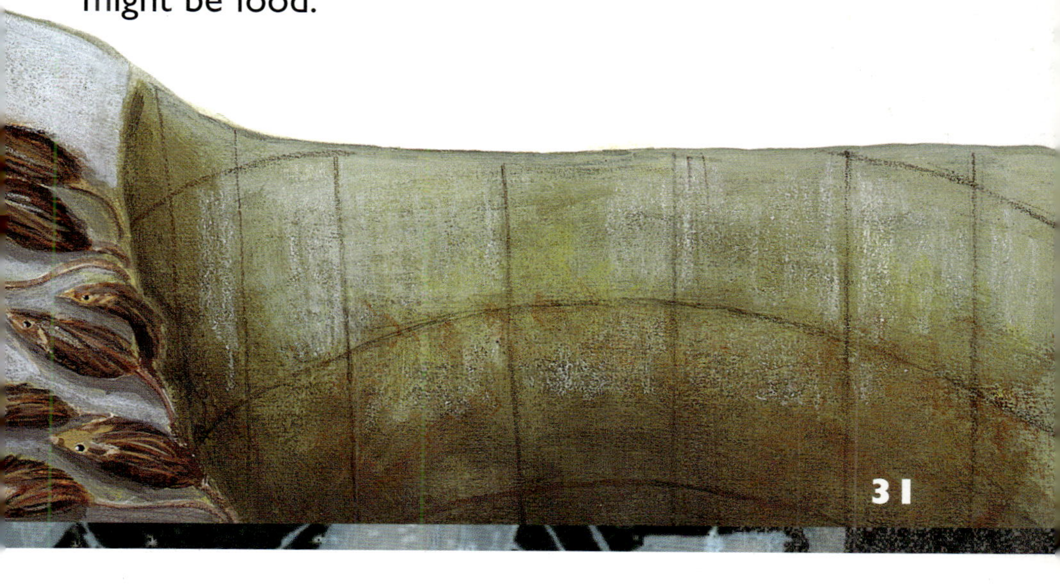

Suddenly, their greediness gave me a plan of escape. I grabbed at the last of the meat. Then, struggling to twist my hand around, I rubbed the meat along the leather strap.

The scent of it brought the rats scurrying all over me. They gnawed at the strap, eager to chew anything that smelt and tasted of meat.

The pendulum's blade hissed loudly across my chest. It cut into the rags I was wearing. Two more swings and it would be at my skin!

Then, the strap came loose. As the pendulum bore down on me, I rolled off the wooden frame and onto the floor. I was safe again.

The rats had bitten through the leather strap – I had escaped death a second time. But my relief was short-lived. I knew that the Inquisition would not allow me a third chance. They would make sure I died, one way or another.

Sure enough, within moments, the final torture began. The metal plates on the walls began to glow; and the smell of hot iron filled the dungeon. The plates were heating up and the eyes of the painted demons shone fiercely. The plates grew hotter and hotter.

The intense heat forced me away from the walls. My torturers were trying to drive me into the middle of the dungeon. The walls seemed to be coming closer. The dungeon was getting smaller, I wasn't imagining it. The walls were moving in.

Either I would burn to death, or fall into the pit! What could I do? I couldn't think. I couldn't move. All I could do was scream with fear. I could stand it no more.

Then, there were voices. Loud voices, outside the dungeon. And a terrible grinding noise inside.

The walls were rushing back. But it was too late. Teetering at the edge of the pit, I slipped and fell...

Suddenly, an arm caught mine. I was pulled to safety.

Only later did I find out that it was a French soldier who had saved my life. The French, bitter enemies of the Spanish, had sent an army to storm the prison. The Inquisition had been defeated.

Dotheboys Hall

scenes from Nicholas Nickleby
By Charles Dickens

dramatised by William Bedford

illustrated by David Roberts

Characters

Mr Wackford Squeers
the bullying Headmaster who runs Dotheboys Hall, a school for unwanted children

Mrs Squeers
the Headmaster's bullying wife

Belling
a new boy

Mr Nicholas Nickleby
Ralph's nephew, an innocent young man

Mr Snawley
a cruel stepfather

Mr Ralph Nickleby
a dishonest lawyer

Waiter
who also reads stage directions in Scene 1

Smike
a kind-hearted boy of nineteen who has been cruelly treated all his life by Wackford and Mrs Squeers

Mobbs
a boy

Bolder
a boy

Cobbey
a boy, who also reads stage directions in Scene 2

Master Squeers
spoiled son of the Squeers, who also reads stage directions in Scene 3

Miss Fanny Squeers
spoiled daughter of the Squeers

Scene 1

one

The Saracen's Head Inn

Squeers (*in a fury*) It's half-past three and no more new boys! What's the world coming to!

Belling (*sneezes*)

Squeers What's that?

Belling (*terrified*) Nothing, please, sir.

Squeers Nothing!

Belling Please, sir, I sneezed.

Squeers Sneezed, did you? Then why did you say "nothing"?

Belling I don't know, sir.

Squeers (*hits Belling hard around the head*) Well, take that!

Belling Ow!

Squeers And don't do it again.

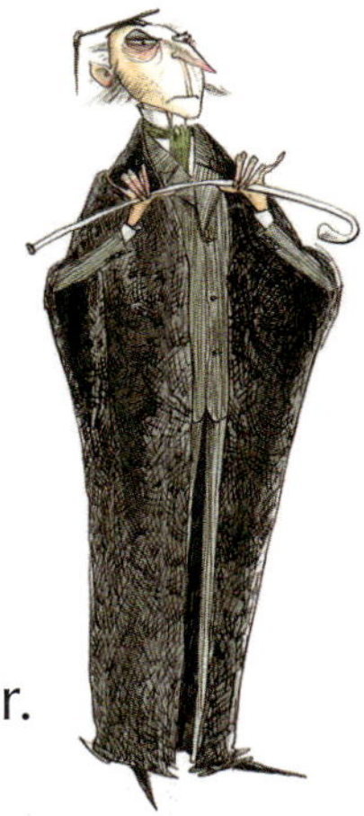

Waiter enters.

Waiter Mr Squeers, there's a gentleman asking for you at the bar.

Squeers A gentleman!

Waiter That's what he looks like, sir.

Squeers Show him in then, boy!

Waiter goes.

Squeers Miserable youth! And you boy, stop snivelling or I'll murder you.

Belling Yes, sir.

Squeers is sitting beside Belling and pretending to be friendly. Mr Snawley and his sons enter.

Squeers My dear, you are leaving your friends and your eyes are full of tears.

Belling Yes, sir.

Squeers But you will have a father in me, and a mother in Mrs Squeers.

Snawley Mr Squeers, I believe?

Squeers It is indeed, sir. I did not see you there.

Snawley You advertised in *The Times* newspaper?

Squeers I did, sir. And these are your sons. How do you do, my young friends?

Snawley My name is Snawley, Mr Squeers. I have been thinking of placing my boys in your school.

Squeers You couldn't do a better thing for them, sir.

Snawley Twenty pounds a year?

Squeers Each.

Snawley It couldn't be done for less?

Squeers Not a penny less.

Snawley They are not great eaters.

Squeers Then we will not be great feeders.

Snawley Could we have a few words aside, Mr Squeers?

They move away so that they can't be heard.

Snawley The thing is, sir, they are not my children. I am their stepfather.

Squeers I understand. A nuisance around the house. An expense you hadn't planned for.

Snawley How long do you keep your boys, Mr Squeers?

Squeers They will need a razor, sir, before the time comes for them to leave.

Snawley No holidays?

Squeers None.

Snawley That's good. No letters home?

Squeers None.

Snawley That suits me. We understand each other, Mr Squeers.

Squeers And always will, Mr Snawley, so long as the bills are paid.

Ralph and Nicholas Nickleby enter, with waiter.

Waiter Two more gentlemen, Mr Squeers.

Squeers Ah ha! Business is looking up!

Ralph Nickleby Mr Squeers?

Squeers That's my name.

Ralph Nickleby My name is Nickleby. This is my nephew, Nicholas Nickleby.

Squeers How do you do, sir?

Nicholas How do you do?

Ralph Nickleby You have been advertising for a teaching assistant, Mr Squeers. My nephew is the man for you.

Squeers Who says so?

Ralph Nickleby I do. Let's talk business, Mr Squeers.

Squeers With all my heart, sir. "Never postpone business" is one of the first things we teach our boys. Master Belling, you must remember that, do you hear?

Belling Yes, sir.

Ralph Nickleby Does he remember it?

Squeers Tell the gentleman, my dear.

Belling Never...

Squeers Very good. Go on.

Belling Never...

Squeers Very good again.

Nicholas Try a word beginning with "P".

Belling Never – perform – business!

Squeers (*aside to Belling sarcastically*) Very good. I'll have the skin off your back for that when I get you home.

Ralph Nickleby My nephew will do for you, Mr Squeers. You heard how he helped the boy.

Squeers I'll pay him five pounds a year and all his food.

Ralph Nickleby That will do him very well.

Squeers Then it will do us well. Be here at seven in the morning, Mr Nickleby. Don't be late. We have a long journey to Yorkshire.

Scene 2
two

Dotheboys Hall

The dormitory of Dotheboys Hall. This is a filthy loft, where all the boys and Nicholas sleep.

Squeers Wake up there! It's past seven o'clock, Nickleby.

Nicholas Has morning come already?

Squeers It has, and it is frosty too. The water pump's frozen. So you can't wash yourself this morning.

Nicholas Not wash myself!

Squeers That's right. Give yourself a bit of a polish. Don't stand staring at me, get a move on.

Mrs Squeers (*in a sickly sweet voice*) Squeersy!

Squeers Come in, my love.

Mrs Squeers What's to do? There's work to be done, Mr Knuckleby.

Nicholas Nickleby, Mrs Squeers.

Mrs Squeers The work won't get done being particular over names.
I've lost the wooden spoon.

Squeers Wooden spoon, my dear?

Mrs Squeers One of the boys must have stolen it.

Squeers Why do you need the wooden spoon, my dear?

Mrs Squeers This is brimstone morning, Squeers. Have you forgotten?

Squeers Ah, so it is. I forgot to mention it, Nickleby. We give the boys medicine to keep them free of colds.

Mrs Squeers Nonsense! We give them brimstone, Mr Knuckleboy, because it spoils their appetites and saves us the cost of breakfast and dinner. Where's that spoon? (*shouting*) Smike!

Smike appears.

Smike (*cringing and fearful*) I'm here, Mrs Squeers.

Mrs Squeers Where've you hidden the wooden spoon?

Smike Please, Mrs...

Squeers Thief!

Mrs Squeers Liar!

Smike It's in your pocket, Mrs Squeers.

Mrs Squeers No it's not. Don't you call me a liar. (*hits Smike hard across the head*) Take that for your trouble.

Nicholas But I see it, Mrs Squeers.

Mrs Squeers Where?

Nicholas In your pocket.

Mrs Squeers You can shut up too, Mr Knuckleboy. Smike, get the children to the schoolroom.

They are in the schoolroom half an hour later. The boys are queuing for their brimstone, which tastes horrible.

Squeers Be quiet, you boys! I'll skin any boy who makes a sound.

Mrs Squeers New boys first. Move, you lazy dogs!

Squeers Isn't she a wonderful woman, Nickleby?

Mobbs Urgghhh!

Nicholas Wonderful, sir.

Squeers She does more for these boys than any mother would do.

Nicholas I can see that, sir.

Cobbey Yerrkkk!

Mrs Squeers That's it! All finished.

Squeers Well done, my dear. Now I'll show you how we go on, Nickleby. We use the practical method of teaching here.

Nicholas Indeed.

Squeers You just watch me. Cobbey?

Cobbey	Yes, sir.
Squeers	What is to clean? Spelt c – l – e – a – n?
Cobbey	To scour, to make bright, sir.
Squeers	Good. When this lesson's over, go and clean some windows, boy.
Cobbey	Yes, sir.
Squeers	Mobbs!
Mobbs	Here, sir.
Squeers	Mobbs. What's a horse? Spelt h – o – r – s – e?
Mobbs	A horse is a beast, sir.
Squeers	Good. When this lesson's done, go and rub my horse down or I'll rub you down.
Mobbs	Yes, sir.
Squeers	What do you think of it, Nickleby?
Nicholas	Very practical, sir.

Squeers It is, it is. Now, letters from home. Another great tradition of Dotheboys Hall, Nickleby.

Nicholas I am pleased to hear it, sir.

Squeers Cobbey!

Cobbey Yes, sir.

Squeers Your grandmother is dead. Your sister sends you a shilling.

Mrs Squeers (*putting it in her pocket*) We'll take care of that for you, Cobbey.

Squeers Bolder!

Bolder Yes, sir.

Squeers Your father's two pounds short of his bill. You can see me afterwards, for a flogging. I'll teach you to have a father who doesn't pay his bills.

Bolder Yes, sir.

Squeers Mobbs!

Mobbs Yes, sir.

Squeers Your stepmother is shocked to hear that you won't eat fat, Mobbs. She asks me to flog you until you learn to eat what you are given. See me afterwards.

Mobbs Yes, sir.

Squeers No more letters. Now, boys, go and draw water from the well. It is washing day tomorrow.

Smike Please, sir.

Squeers What is it now, Smike?

Smike Please, sir, is there anything for me, sir?

Squeers What's that, boy?

Smike Any letter for me, sir?

Squeers Nobody is ever going to write to you, Smike. Mrs Squeers and I are your family. Now go and wait with Mobbs. You can have a flogging for your cheek!

Scene 3

three

Smike

Some weeks later. The bullying has continued. Smike and Nicholas have become close. They are alone in the dormitory.

Nicholas You poor boy.

Smike Do not be kind to me, sir. I can't bear kindness. It makes me cry.

Nicholas Don't cry, Smike.

Smike I can't help it, sir. They are so hard on me.

Nicholas They are worse than hard. They are cruel.

Smike They will kill me one day. I know they will.

Nicholas I will protect you as long as I am here, Smike.

Smike Are you going to leave?

Nicholas I don't know.

Smike Oh, please say you won't leave.

Nicholas I can't, Smike. I may be driven out into the world by all this cruelty.

Smike Is the world as bad and dismal as this place?

Nicholas No, Smike, it isn't.

Smike If I followed you, would I meet you there? If you were to go?

Nicholas Yes, Smike, but...

Smike Say I would be sure to find you.

Nicholas You would, and I would help you and not bring fresh sorrow on you.

Smike Oh thank you, sir.

A few days later at dawn. In the dormitory, Nicholas and the boys are asleep.

Squeers Nickleby! Are you going to sleep all day?

Mrs Squeers Wake up, you lazy dogs!

Nicholas We are coming, sir.

Squeers Where's that Smike?

Nicholas I don't know, sir.

Squeers Smike!

Mrs Squeers Do you want another flogging, Smike?

Nicholas He's not here, sir.

Squeers Don't tell me a lie. He is.

Nicholas He is not!

Mrs Squeers Squeersy, don't listen to that Knuckleboy. He's hidden the boy.

Squeers Where have you hidden him, Nickleby?

Nicholas I have not seen him, sir.

Mrs Squeers He's a liar, Squeersy. Take no notice. We must find Smike. Sound the alarm. Find him!

Squeers And skin him alive when we do!

Nicholas (*under his breath*) I hope you never do.

The classroom two days later. The boys wait with Nicholas. Squeers and his wife and children enter.

Squeers Is every boy here?

Master Squeers They're all here, Father.

Mrs Squeers Snivelling creatures.

Squeers You boys, sit down. Nickleby, you too, sir!

Nicholas I will stand.

Mrs Squeers Fetch the boy, Squeersy.

Squeers (*drags Smike into the classroom*) Here he is. Don't cry, boy. You'll have something to cry about before long. Have you got anything to say for yourself?

Smike Spare me, sir!

Mrs Squeers Spare me! Listen to the wretched boy.

Squeers I'll spare you, boy. I'll spare the last breath of your life so I can thrash you again in the morning.

Master Squeers Hit him, Father.

Fanny Squeers Beat him, Father.

Smike Oh sir, please spare me.

Squeers (*all the time hitting Smike*) Take that you ungrateful wretch. And that, and that, and that…

Smike Help me, help me. Please somebody help me.

Mrs Squeers You nasty, ungrateful, pig-headed, brutish, obstinate, sneaking dog!

Squeers (*still hitting Smike*) And that, and that, and that...

Nicholas (*shouting*) Stop!

Squeers Who cried stop?

Nicholas I did. This must not go on.

Squeers Must not go on?

Nicholas No!

Squeers Get away, you beggar!

Nicholas I will not stand by and watch this cruelty.

Squeers Stand back or you will get a flogging yourself.

Nicholas Touch that boy again, and you will regret it, Squeers.

Mrs Squeers (*to Nicholas*) Beast.

Master Squeers (*to Nicholas*) Beggar.

Fanny Squeers (*to Nicholas*) Brute.

Nicholas (*hitting Squeers and rescuing Smike*) Take that, and that, and that...

Mrs Squeers Squeersy! Are you hurt?

Master Squeers Poor Father.

Fanny Squeers Dear Father.

Nicholas takes Smike by the hand.

Nicholas Come with me, Smike.

Smike Where, sir?

Nicholas Out into the world. To freedom.